Daily Wellness Journal

THIS JOURNAL BELONGS TO:

_____

📞 _____

✉️ _____

▤ _____

_____

SHOP MORE NOTEBOOKS
& OTHER STATIONERY GOODS!

MODERNPINKPAPER.COM

How to use; Explained

WAKE UP - *Logging your wake up time can be great insight to how it effects your mood and health throughout the day.*

BED TIME - *Logging your bed time can be great insight to how it effects your mood and health the following day.*

SLEEP (HRS) - *Logging your sleep hours can be great insight to how it effects your mood and health throughout the day. This number should reflect how many hours you slept the night before.*

WHAT I ATE TODAY - *Logging your food intake can be great insight to how it effects your mood and health throughout the day.*

EXERCISE LOG - *Logging your exercise each day can be great insight to how it effects your mood and health throughout the day.*

PERSONAL ACTIVITIES - *Log your activities that you do for yourself, such as things you enjoy and self care. Health and wellness also comes from how you spend your time.*

MOOD TRACKER - *Keep track of your mood throughout the day – this is a great way to see how your mood may be effected by the things you do.*

CREATE YOUR OWN EMOJI MOOD LEGEND

example

angry

WATER INTAKE - *Keep track of how much water you drink by coloring in the cups or writing the amount of ozs you consumed.*

FAMILY ACTIVITIES - *Jot down the activities you do with your family. Health and wellness also comes from how you spend your time.*

WHAT ARE YOU GRATEFUL FOR TODAY? - *Practicing gratitude each day will do wonders for your health. Jot anything that comes to mind.*

WHAT WOULD'VE MADE TODAY BETTER? - *Practicing gratitude each day will do wonders for your health. Jot anything that comes to mind.*

NOTES: - *Any additional notes you want to make that you believe to be important to note about your health and wellness for that day.*

How to use; Example

DATE: 8/13/18

WAKE UP	BED TIME	SLEEP (HRS)
8:20 am	10:30 pm	8.5 hours

WHAT I ATE TODAY

B oatmeal
L avocado toast
D chicken & rice
S pretzels

EXERCISE LOG

30 min walking
5 stretching

PERSONAL ACTIVITIES

reading for 30m
bubble bath

MOOD TRACKER

😊 MORNING
😐 AFTERNOON
☹️ NIGHT

WATER INTAKE

FAMILY ACTIVITIES

played bingo with
kids & went toy
shopping with them

WHAT ARE YOU GRATEFUL FOR TODAY?

my health! I haven't had to
see the doctor for any
illness for over 6 years

NOTES:

received bad news from my
mom, that's why my mood at
night changed.

WHAT WOULD'VE MADE TODAY BETTER?

more time to walk - was cut
short due to kids schedule

Daily Wellness Journal

DATE: _____

WAKE UP	BED TIME	SLEEP (HRS)
_____	_____	_____

WHAT I ATE TODAY	EXERCISE LOG	PERSONAL ACTIVITIES
B _____	_____	_____
L _____	_____	_____
D _____	_____	_____
S _____	_____	_____

MOOD TRACKER

◯ MORNING
◯ AFTERNOON
◯ NIGHT

WATER INTAKE

FAMILY ACTIVITIES

_____
_____
_____

WHAT ARE YOU GRATEFUL FOR TODAY?

_____
_____
_____
_____

WHAT WOULD'VE MADE TODAY BETTER?

_____
_____
_____

NOTES:

_____
_____
_____
_____
_____
_____
_____
_____

Daily Wellness Journal

DATE: _____

WAKE UP	BED TIME	SLEEP (HRS)
_____	_____	_____

WHAT I ATE TODAY / EXERCISE LOG / PERSONAL ACTIVITIES

WHAT I ATE TODAY	EXERCISE LOG	PERSONAL ACTIVITIES
B _____	_____	_____
L _____	_____	_____
D _____	_____	_____
S _____	_____	_____

MOOD TRACKER / WATER INTAKE / FAMILY ACTIVITIES

MOOD TRACKER
- ◯ MORNING
- ◯ AFTERNOON
- ◯ NIGHT

WATER INTAKE

FAMILY ACTIVITIES
_____
_____
_____

WHAT ARE YOU GRATEFUL FOR TODAY?

_____
_____
_____
_____

WHAT WOULD'VE MADE TODAY BETTER?

_____
_____
_____

NOTES:
_____
_____
_____
_____
_____
_____
_____

Daily Wellness Journal

DATE: _____

WAKE UP	BED TIME	SLEEP (HRS)
_____	_____	_____

WHAT I ATE TODAY	EXERCISE LOG	PERSONAL ACTIVITIES
B _____	_____	_____
L _____	_____	_____
D _____	_____	_____
S _____	_____	_____

MOOD TRACKER

◯ MORNING

◯ AFTERNOON

◯ NIGHT

WATER INTAKE

FAMILY ACTIVITIES

_____

_____

_____

WHAT ARE YOU GRATEFUL FOR TODAY?

_____

_____

_____

_____

WHAT WOULD'VE MADE TODAY BETTER?

_____

_____

_____

_____

NOTES:

_____

_____

_____

_____

_____

_____

_____

_____

Daily Wellness Journal

DATE: _____

WAKE UP	BED TIME	SLEEP (HRS)
_____	_____	_____

WHAT I ATE TODAY   EXERCISE LOG   PERSONAL ACTIVITIES

B _____   _____   _____

L _____   _____   _____

D _____   _____   _____

S _____   _____   _____

MOOD TRACKER   WATER INTAKE   FAMILY ACTIVITIES

◯ MORNING

◯ AFTERNOON   _____

◯ NIGHT   _____

WHAT ARE YOU GRATEFUL FOR TODAY?   NOTES:

_____   _____

_____   _____

_____   _____

_____   _____

WHAT WOULD'VE MADE TODAY BETTER?   _____

_____   _____

_____   _____

_____   _____

Daily Wellness Journal

DATE: _____

WAKE UP	BED TIME	SLEEP (HRS)
_____	_____	_____

WHAT I ATE TODAY	EXERCISE LOG	PERSONAL ACTIVITIES
B _____	_____	_____
L _____	_____	_____
D _____	_____	_____
S _____	_____	_____

MOOD TRACKER

◯ MORNING

◯ AFTERNOON

◯ NIGHT

WATER INTAKE

FAMILY ACTIVITIES

_____

_____

_____

WHAT ARE YOU GRATEFUL FOR TODAY?

_____

_____

_____

_____

WHAT WOULD'VE MADE TODAY BETTER?

_____

_____

_____

NOTES:

_____

_____

_____

_____

_____

_____

_____

_____

_____

_____

Daily Wellness Journal

DATE: _____

WAKE UP	BED TIME	SLEEP (HRS)
_____	_____	_____

WHAT I ATE TODAY

B _____

L _____

D _____

S _____

EXERCISE LOG

_____

_____

_____

_____

PERSONAL ACTIVITIES

_____

_____

_____

_____

MOOD TRACKER

◯ MORNING

◯ AFTERNOON

◯ NIGHT

WATER INTAKE

FAMILY ACTIVITIES

_____

_____

_____

WHAT ARE YOU GRATEFUL FOR TODAY?

_____

_____

_____

_____

WHAT WOULD'VE MADE TODAY BETTER?

_____

_____

_____

NOTES:

_____

_____

_____

_____

_____

_____

_____

_____

Daily Wellness Journal

DATE: _____

WAKE UP	BED TIME	SLEEP (HRS)
_____	_____	_____

WHAT I ATE TODAY   EXERCISE LOG   PERSONAL ACTIVITIES

B _____   _____   _____

L _____   _____   _____

D _____   _____   _____

S _____   _____   _____

MOOD TRACKER   WATER INTAKE   FAMILY ACTIVITIES

◯ MORNING

◯ AFTERNOON

◯ NIGHT

WHAT ARE YOU GRATEFUL FOR TODAY?

_____

_____

_____

NOTES:

_____

_____

_____

_____

_____

WHAT WOULD'VE MADE TODAY BETTER?

_____

_____

_____

Daily Wellness Journal

DATE: _____

WAKE UP	BED TIME	SLEEP (HRS)
_____	_____	_____

WHAT I ATE TODAY

B _____

L _____

D _____

S _____

EXERCISE LOG

_____

_____

_____

_____

PERSONAL ACTIVITIES

_____

_____

_____

_____

MOOD TRACKER

○ MORNING

○ AFTERNOON

○ NIGHT

WATER INTAKE

FAMILY ACTIVITIES

_____

_____

_____

WHAT ARE YOU GRATEFUL FOR TODAY?

_____

_____

_____

_____

WHAT WOULD'VE MADE TODAY BETTER?

_____

_____

_____

_____

NOTES:

_____

_____

_____

_____

_____

_____

_____

_____

Daily Wellness Journal

DATE: _____

WAKE UP	BED TIME	SLEEP (HRS)
_____	_____	_____

WHAT I ATE TODAY	EXERCISE LOG	PERSONAL ACTIVITIES
B _____	_____	_____
L _____	_____	_____
D _____	_____	_____
S _____	_____	_____

MOOD TRACKER	WATER INTAKE	FAMILY ACTIVITIES
◯ MORNING		_____
◯ AFTERNOON		_____
◯ NIGHT		_____

WHAT ARE YOU GRATEFUL FOR TODAY?

_____

_____

_____

_____

NOTES:

_____

_____

_____

_____

_____

_____

WHAT WOULD'VE MADE TODAY BETTER?

_____

_____

_____

Daily Wellness Journal

DATE: _____

WAKE UP	BED TIME	SLEEP (HRS)
_____	_____	_____

WHAT I ATE TODAY	EXERCISE LOG	PERSONAL ACTIVITIES
B _____	_____	_____
L _____	_____	_____
D _____	_____	_____
S _____	_____	_____

MOOD TRACKER

- ◯ MORNING
- ◯ AFTERNOON
- ◯ NIGHT

WATER INTAKE

FAMILY ACTIVITIES

_____
_____
_____

WHAT ARE YOU GRATEFUL FOR TODAY?

_____
_____
_____
_____

WHAT WOULD'VE MADE TODAY BETTER?

_____
_____
_____

NOTES:

_____
_____
_____
_____
_____
_____
_____
_____
_____

Daily Wellness Journal

DATE: _____

WAKE UP	BED TIME	SLEEP (HRS)
_____	_____	_____

WHAT I ATE TODAY	EXERCISE LOG	PERSONAL ACTIVITIES
B _____	_____	_____
L _____	_____	_____
D _____	_____	_____
S _____	_____	_____

MOOD TRACKER	WATER INTAKE	FAMILY ACTIVITIES
◯ MORNING		_____
◯ AFTERNOON		_____
◯ NIGHT		_____

WHAT ARE YOU GRATEFUL FOR TODAY?

_____

_____

_____

_____

NOTES:

_____

_____

_____

_____

WHAT WOULD'VE MADE TODAY BETTER?

_____

_____

_____

Daily Wellness Journal

DATE: _____

WAKE UP	BED TIME	SLEEP (HRS)
_____	_____	_____

WHAT I ATE TODAY	EXERCISE LOG	PERSONAL ACTIVITIES
B _____	_____	_____
L _____	_____	_____
D _____	_____	_____
S _____	_____	_____

MOOD TRACKER

- ◯ MORNING
- ◯ AFTERNOON
- ◯ NIGHT

WATER INTAKE

FAMILY ACTIVITIES

_____

_____

_____

WHAT ARE YOU GRATEFUL FOR TODAY?

_____

_____

_____

WHAT WOULD'VE MADE TODAY BETTER?

_____

_____

_____

NOTES:

_____

_____

_____

_____

_____

_____

_____

Daily Wellness Journal

DATE: _____

WAKE UP	BED TIME	SLEEP (HRS)
_____	_____	_____

WHAT I ATE TODAY	EXERCISE LOG	PERSONAL ACTIVITIES
B _____	_____	_____
L _____	_____	_____
D _____	_____	_____
S _____	_____	_____

MOOD TRACKER

◯ MORNING

◯ AFTERNOON

◯ NIGHT

WATER INTAKE

FAMILY ACTIVITIES

_____

_____

_____

_____

WHAT ARE YOU GRATEFUL FOR TODAY?

_____

_____

_____

_____

WHAT WOULD'VE MADE TODAY BETTER?

_____

_____

_____

NOTES:

_____

_____

_____

_____

_____

_____

_____

_____

_____

Daily Wellness Journal

DATE: _____

WAKE UP	BED TIME	SLEEP (HRS)
_____	_____	_____

WHAT I ATE TODAY	EXERCISE LOG	PERSONAL ACTIVITIES
B _____	_____	_____
L _____	_____	_____
D _____	_____	_____
S _____	_____	_____

MOOD TRACKER

- ◯ MORNING
- ◯ AFTERNOON
- ◯ NIGHT

WATER INTAKE

FAMILY ACTIVITIES

_____

_____

_____

WHAT ARE YOU GRATEFUL FOR TODAY?

_____

_____

_____

_____

WHAT WOULD'VE MADE TODAY BETTER?

_____

_____

_____

NOTES:

_____

_____

_____

_____

_____

_____

_____

_____

_____

Daily Wellness Journal

DATE: _____

WAKE UP	BED TIME	SLEEP (HRS)
_____	_____	_____

WHAT I ATE TODAY   EXERCISE LOG   PERSONAL ACTIVITIES

B _____   _____   _____

L _____   _____   _____

D _____   _____   _____

S _____   _____   _____

MOOD TRACKER   WATER INTAKE   FAMILY ACTIVITIES

◯ MORNING

◯ AFTERNOON

◯ NIGHT

WHAT ARE YOU GRATEFUL FOR TODAY?

_____

_____

_____

_____

WHAT WOULD'VE MADE TODAY BETTER?

_____

_____

_____

NOTES:

_____

_____

_____

_____

_____

_____

_____

Daily Wellness Journal

DATE: _____

WAKE UP	BED TIME	SLEEP (HRS)
_____	_____	_____

WHAT I ATE TODAY / EXERCISE LOG / PERSONAL ACTIVITIES

WHAT I ATE TODAY	EXERCISE LOG	PERSONAL ACTIVITIES
B _____	_____	_____
L _____	_____	_____
D _____	_____	_____
S _____	_____	_____

MOOD TRACKER / WATER INTAKE / FAMILY ACTIVITIES

MOOD TRACKER
- ◯ MORNING
- ◯ AFTERNOON
- ◯ NIGHT

WATER INTAKE

FAMILY ACTIVITIES
_____
_____
_____

WHAT ARE YOU GRATEFUL FOR TODAY?

_____
_____
_____
_____

WHAT WOULD'VE MADE TODAY BETTER?

_____
_____
_____
_____

NOTES:

_____
_____
_____
_____
_____
_____
_____
_____

Daily Wellness Journal

DATE: _____

WAKE UP	BED TIME	SLEEP (HRS)
_____	_____	_____

WHAT I ATE TODAY | EXERCISE LOG | PERSONAL ACTIVITIES

B _____

L _____

D _____

S _____

MOOD TRACKER

◯ MORNING

◯ AFTERNOON

◯ NIGHT

WATER INTAKE

FAMILY ACTIVITIES

WHAT ARE YOU GRATEFUL FOR TODAY?

_____

_____

_____

_____

WHAT WOULD'VE MADE TODAY BETTER?

_____

_____

_____

NOTES:

_____

_____

_____

_____

_____

_____

_____

Daily Wellness Journal

DATE: _____

WAKE UP	BED TIME	SLEEP (HRS)
_____	_____	_____

WHAT I ATE TODAY

B _____

L _____

D _____

S _____

EXERCISE LOG

_____

_____

_____

_____

PERSONAL ACTIVITIES

_____

_____

_____

_____

MOOD TRACKER

◯ MORNING

◯ AFTERNOON

◯ NIGHT

WATER INTAKE

FAMILY ACTIVITIES

_____

_____

_____

WHAT ARE YOU GRATEFUL FOR TODAY?

_____

_____

_____

_____

WHAT WOULD'VE MADE TODAY BETTER?

_____

_____

_____

NOTES:

_____

_____

_____

_____

_____

_____

_____

_____

Daily Wellness Journal

DATE: _____

WAKE UP	BED TIME	SLEEP (HRS)
_____	_____	_____

WHAT I ATE TODAY

B _____

L _____

D _____

S _____

EXERCISE LOG

_____

_____

_____

_____

PERSONAL ACTIVITIES

_____

_____

_____

_____

MOOD TRACKER

◯ MORNING

◯ AFTERNOON

◯ NIGHT

WATER INTAKE

▢ ▢ ▢ ▢

▢ ▢ ▢ ▢

FAMILY ACTIVITIES

_____

_____

_____

WHAT ARE YOU GRATEFUL FOR TODAY?

_____

_____

_____

_____

WHAT WOULD'VE MADE TODAY BETTER?

_____

_____

_____

NOTES:

_____

_____

_____

_____

_____

_____

_____

_____

Daily Wellness Journal

DATE: _____

WAKE UP	BED TIME	SLEEP (HRS)
_____	_____	_____

WHAT I ATE TODAY	EXERCISE LOG	PERSONAL ACTIVITIES
B _____	_____	_____
L _____	_____	_____
D _____	_____	_____
S _____	_____	_____

MOOD TRACKER

- ◯ MORNING
- ◯ AFTERNOON
- ◯ NIGHT

WATER INTAKE

▽ ▽ ▽ ▽
▽ ▽ ▽ ▽

FAMILY ACTIVITIES

_____

_____

_____

WHAT ARE YOU GRATEFUL FOR TODAY?

_____

_____

_____

_____

WHAT WOULD'VE MADE TODAY BETTER?

_____

_____

NOTES:

_____

_____

_____

_____

_____

_____

_____

_____

_____

Daily Wellness Journal

DATE: _____

WAKE UP	BED TIME	SLEEP (HRS)
_____	_____	_____

WHAT I ATE TODAY	EXERCISE LOG	PERSONAL ACTIVITIES
B _____	_____	_____
L _____	_____	_____
D _____	_____	_____
S _____	_____	_____

MOOD TRACKER
◯ MORNING
◯ AFTERNOON
◯ NIGHT

WATER INTAKE

FAMILY ACTIVITIES
_____
_____
_____

WHAT ARE YOU GRATEFUL FOR TODAY?

_____
_____
_____
_____

NOTES:

_____
_____
_____
_____
_____
_____

WHAT WOULD'VE MADE TODAY BETTER?

_____
_____
_____

Daily Wellness Journal

DATE: _____

WAKE UP	BED TIME	SLEEP (HRS)
_____	_____	_____

WHAT I ATE TODAY	EXERCISE LOG	PERSONAL ACTIVITIES
B _____	_____	_____
L _____	_____	_____
D _____	_____	_____
S _____	_____	_____

MOOD TRACKER

◯ MORNING

◯ AFTERNOON

◯ NIGHT

WATER INTAKE

FAMILY ACTIVITIES

_____

_____

_____

WHAT ARE YOU GRATEFUL FOR TODAY?

_____

_____

_____

WHAT WOULD'VE MADE TODAY BETTER?

_____

_____

_____

NOTES:

_____

_____

_____

_____

_____

_____

_____

_____

Daily Wellness Journal

DATE: _____

WAKE UP	BED TIME	SLEEP (HRS)
_____	_____	_____

WHAT I ATE TODAY	EXERCISE LOG	PERSONAL ACTIVITIES
B _____	_____	_____
L _____	_____	_____
D _____	_____	_____
S _____	_____	_____

MOOD TRACKER
◯ MORNING
◯ AFTERNOON
◯ NIGHT

WATER INTAKE

FAMILY ACTIVITIES
_____
_____
_____

WHAT ARE YOU GRATEFUL FOR TODAY?
_____
_____
_____
_____

NOTES:
_____
_____
_____
_____
_____
_____

WHAT WOULD'VE MADE TODAY BETTER?
_____
_____
_____

Daily Wellness Journal

DATE: _____

WAKE UP	BED TIME	SLEEP (HRS)
_____	_____	_____

WHAT I ATE TODAY

B _____

L _____

D _____

S _____

EXERCISE LOG

_____

_____

_____

_____

PERSONAL ACTIVITIES

_____

_____

_____

_____

MOOD TRACKER

◯ MORNING

◯ AFTERNOON

◯ NIGHT

WATER INTAKE

FAMILY ACTIVITIES

_____

_____

_____

WHAT ARE YOU GRATEFUL FOR TODAY?

_____

_____

_____

_____

WHAT WOULD'VE MADE TODAY BETTER?

_____

_____

_____

_____

NOTES:

_____

_____

_____

_____

_____

_____

_____

_____

_____

Daily Wellness Journal

DATE: _____

WAKE UP	BED TIME	SLEEP (HRS)
_____	_____	_____

WHAT I ATE TODAY

B _____

L _____

D _____

S _____

EXERCISE LOG

_____

_____

_____

_____

PERSONAL ACTIVITIES

_____

_____

_____

_____

MOOD TRACKER

◯ MORNING

◯ AFTERNOON

◯ NIGHT

WATER INTAKE

FAMILY ACTIVITIES

_____

_____

_____

WHAT ARE YOU GRATEFUL FOR TODAY?

_____

_____

_____

_____

WHAT WOULD'VE MADE TODAY BETTER?

_____

_____

_____

NOTES:

_____

_____

_____

_____

_____

_____

_____

Daily Wellness Journal

DATE: _____

WAKE UP	BED TIME	SLEEP (HRS)
_____	_____	_____

WHAT I ATE TODAY

B _____

L _____

D _____

S _____

EXERCISE LOG

_____

_____

_____

_____

PERSONAL ACTIVITIES

_____

_____

_____

_____

MOOD TRACKER

◯ MORNING

◯ AFTERNOON

◯ NIGHT

WATER INTAKE

FAMILY ACTIVITIES

_____

_____

_____

WHAT ARE YOU GRATEFUL FOR TODAY?

_____

_____

_____

_____

NOTES:

_____

_____

_____

_____

_____

WHAT WOULD'VE MADE TODAY BETTER?

_____

_____

_____

Daily Wellness Journal

DATE: _____

WAKE UP	BED TIME	SLEEP (HRS)
_____	_____	_____

WHAT I ATE TODAY	EXERCISE LOG	PERSONAL ACTIVITIES
B _____	_____	_____
L _____	_____	_____
D _____	_____	_____
S _____	_____	_____

MOOD TRACKER
◯ MORNING
◯ AFTERNOON
◯ NIGHT

WATER INTAKE

FAMILY ACTIVITIES
_____
_____
_____

WHAT ARE YOU GRATEFUL FOR TODAY?
_____
_____
_____
_____

NOTES:
_____
_____
_____
_____
_____
_____

WHAT WOULD'VE MADE TODAY BETTER?
_____
_____
_____

Daily Wellness Journal

DATE: _____

WAKE UP	BED TIME	SLEEP (HRS)
_____	_____	_____

WHAT I ATE TODAY	EXERCISE LOG	PERSONAL ACTIVITIES
B _____	_____	_____
L _____	_____	_____
D _____	_____	_____
S _____	_____	_____

MOOD TRACKER

◯ MORNING
◯ AFTERNOON
◯ NIGHT

WATER INTAKE

FAMILY ACTIVITIES

_____
_____
_____
_____

WHAT ARE YOU GRATEFUL FOR TODAY?

_____
_____
_____

NOTES:

_____
_____
_____
_____
_____
_____
_____

WHAT WOULD'VE MADE TODAY BETTER?

_____
_____
_____

Daily Wellness Journal

DATE: _____

WAKE UP	BED TIME	SLEEP (HRS)
_____	_____	_____

WHAT I ATE TODAY

B _____

L _____

D _____

S _____

EXERCISE LOG

_____

_____

_____

_____

PERSONAL ACTIVITIES

_____

_____

_____

_____

MOOD TRACKER

○ MORNING

○ AFTERNOON

○ NIGHT

WATER INTAKE

FAMILY ACTIVITIES

_____

_____

_____

WHAT ARE YOU GRATEFUL FOR TODAY?

_____

_____

_____

_____

WHAT WOULD'VE MADE TODAY BETTER?

_____

_____

_____

NOTES:

_____

_____

_____

_____

_____

_____

_____

_____

Daily Wellness Journal

DATE: _____

WAKE UP	BED TIME	SLEEP (HRS)
_____	_____	_____

WHAT I ATE TODAY	EXERCISE LOG	PERSONAL ACTIVITIES
B _____	_____	_____
L _____	_____	_____
D _____	_____	_____
S _____	_____	_____

MOOD TRACKER

○ MORNING
○ AFTERNOON
○ NIGHT

WATER INTAKE

FAMILY ACTIVITIES

_____

_____

_____

WHAT ARE YOU GRATEFUL FOR TODAY?

_____

_____

_____

_____

NOTES:

_____

_____

_____

_____

WHAT WOULD'VE MADE TODAY BETTER?

_____

_____

_____

_____

Daily Wellness Journal

DATE: _____

WAKE UP	BED TIME	SLEEP (HRS)
_____	_____	_____

WHAT I ATE TODAY EXERCISE LOG PERSONAL ACTIVITIES

B _____   _____   _____

L _____   _____   _____

D _____   _____   _____

S _____   _____   _____

MOOD TRACKER   WATER INTAKE   FAMILY ACTIVITIES

◯ MORNING

◯ AFTERNOON

◯ NIGHT

_____

_____

_____

WHAT ARE YOU GRATEFUL FOR TODAY?   NOTES:

_____   _____

_____   _____

_____   _____

_____   _____

WHAT WOULD'VE MADE TODAY BETTER?   _____

_____   _____

_____   _____

_____   _____

Daily Wellness Journal

DATE: _____

WAKE UP	BED TIME	SLEEP (HRS)
_____	_____	_____

WHAT I ATE TODAY

B _____

L _____

D _____

S _____

EXERCISE LOG

_____

_____

_____

_____

PERSONAL ACTIVITIES

_____

_____

_____

_____

MOOD TRACKER

◯ MORNING

◯ AFTERNOON

◯ NIGHT

WATER INTAKE

FAMILY ACTIVITIES

_____

_____

_____

WHAT ARE YOU GRATEFUL FOR TODAY?

_____

_____

_____

_____

WHAT WOULD'VE MADE TODAY BETTER?

_____

_____

_____

NOTES:

_____

_____

_____

_____

_____

_____

_____

_____

Daily Wellness Journal

DATE: _____

WAKE UP	BED TIME	SLEEP (HRS)
_____	_____	_____

WHAT I ATE TODAY

B _____

L _____

D _____

S _____

EXERCISE LOG

_____

_____

_____

_____

PERSONAL ACTIVITIES

_____

_____

_____

_____

MOOD TRACKER

◯ MORNING

◯ AFTERNOON

◯ NIGHT

WATER INTAKE

FAMILY ACTIVITIES

_____

_____

_____

WHAT ARE YOU GRATEFUL FOR TODAY?

_____

_____

_____

_____

WHAT WOULD'VE MADE TODAY BETTER?

_____

_____

_____

NOTES:

_____

_____

_____

_____

_____

_____

_____

_____

_____

Daily Wellness Journal

DATE: _____

WAKE UP	BED TIME	SLEEP (HRS)
_____	_____	_____

WHAT I ATE TODAY | EXERCISE LOG | PERSONAL ACTIVITIES

B _____ _____ _____

L _____ _____ _____

D _____ _____ _____

S _____ _____ _____

MOOD TRACKER | WATER INTAKE | FAMILY ACTIVITIES

○ MORNING

○ AFTERNOON

○ NIGHT

WHAT ARE YOU GRATEFUL FOR TODAY?

_____

_____

_____

WHAT WOULD'VE MADE TODAY BETTER?

_____

_____

_____

NOTES:

_____

_____

_____

_____

_____

_____

Daily Wellness Journal

DATE: _____

WAKE UP	BED TIME	SLEEP (HRS)
_____	_____	_____

WHAT I ATE TODAY

B _____

L _____

D _____

S _____

EXERCISE LOG

_____

_____

_____

_____

PERSONAL ACTIVITIES

_____

_____

_____

_____

MOOD TRACKER

◯ MORNING

◯ AFTERNOON

◯ NIGHT

WATER INTAKE

FAMILY ACTIVITIES

_____

_____

_____

WHAT ARE YOU GRATEFUL FOR TODAY?

_____

_____

_____

_____

WHAT WOULD'VE MADE TODAY BETTER?

_____

_____

_____

NOTES:

_____

_____

_____

_____

_____

_____

_____

_____

Daily Wellness Journal

DATE: _____

WAKE UP	BED TIME	SLEEP (HRS)
_____	_____	_____

WHAT I ATE TODAY	EXERCISE LOG	PERSONAL ACTIVITIES
B _____	_____	_____
L _____	_____	_____
D _____	_____	_____
S _____	_____	_____

MOOD TRACKER
- ◯ MORNING
- ◯ AFTERNOON
- ◯ NIGHT

WATER INTAKE

FAMILY ACTIVITIES

_____

_____

_____

WHAT ARE YOU GRATEFUL FOR TODAY?

_____

_____

_____

_____

WHAT WOULD'VE MADE TODAY BETTER?

_____

_____

_____

NOTES:

_____

_____

_____

_____

_____

_____

_____

_____

Daily Wellness Journal

DATE: _____

WAKE UP	BED TIME	SLEEP (HRS)
_____	_____	_____

WHAT I ATE TODAY	EXERCISE LOG	PERSONAL ACTIVITIES
B _____	_____	_____
L _____	_____	_____
D _____	_____	_____
S _____	_____	_____

MOOD TRACKER	WATER INTAKE	FAMILY ACTIVITIES
◯ MORNING		_____
◯ AFTERNOON		_____
◯ NIGHT		_____

WHAT ARE YOU GRATEFUL FOR TODAY?

_____

_____

_____

_____

WHAT WOULD'VE MADE TODAY BETTER?

_____

_____

_____

NOTES:

_____

_____

_____

_____

_____

_____

_____

_____

Daily Wellness Journal

DATE: _____

WAKE UP	BED TIME	SLEEP (HRS)
_____	_____	_____

WHAT I ATE TODAY	EXERCISE LOG	PERSONAL ACTIVITIES
B _____	_____	_____
L _____	_____	_____
D _____	_____	_____
S _____	_____	_____

MOOD TRACKER

- ◯ MORNING
- ◯ AFTERNOON
- ◯ NIGHT

WATER INTAKE

FAMILY ACTIVITIES

_____

_____

_____

WHAT ARE YOU GRATEFUL FOR TODAY?

_____

_____

_____

_____

WHAT WOULD'VE MADE TODAY BETTER?

_____

_____

_____

NOTES:

_____

_____

_____

_____

_____

_____

_____

_____

Daily Wellness Journal

DATE: _____

WAKE UP	BED TIME	SLEEP (HRS)
_____	_____	_____

WHAT I ATE TODAY	EXERCISE LOG	PERSONAL ACTIVITIES
B _____	_____	_____
L _____	_____	_____
D _____	_____	_____
S _____	_____	_____

MOOD TRACKER

◯ MORNING

◯ AFTERNOON

◯ NIGHT

WATER INTAKE

FAMILY ACTIVITIES

_____

_____

_____

WHAT ARE YOU GRATEFUL FOR TODAY?

_____

_____

_____

WHAT WOULD'VE MADE TODAY BETTER?

_____

_____

NOTES:

_____

_____

_____

_____

_____

_____

_____

Daily Wellness Journal

DATE: _____

WAKE UP	BED TIME	SLEEP (HRS)
_____	_____	_____

WHAT I ATE TODAY	EXERCISE LOG	PERSONAL ACTIVITIES
B _____	_____	_____
L _____	_____	_____
D _____	_____	_____
S _____	_____	_____

MOOD TRACKER

◯ MORNING

◯ AFTERNOON

◯ NIGHT

WATER INTAKE

FAMILY ACTIVITIES

_____

_____

_____

WHAT ARE YOU GRATEFUL FOR TODAY?

_____

_____

_____

_____

NOTES:

_____

_____

_____

_____

_____

WHAT WOULD'VE MADE TODAY BETTER?

_____

_____

_____

_____

Daily Wellness Journal

DATE: _____

WAKE UP	BED TIME	SLEEP (HRS)
_____	_____	_____

WHAT I ATE TODAY

B _____

L _____

D _____

S _____

EXERCISE LOG

_____

_____

_____

_____

PERSONAL ACTIVITIES

_____

_____

_____

_____

MOOD TRACKER

◯ MORNING

◯ AFTERNOON

◯ NIGHT

WATER INTAKE

FAMILY ACTIVITIES

_____

_____

_____

WHAT ARE YOU GRATEFUL FOR TODAY?

_____

_____

_____

_____

WHAT WOULD'VE MADE TODAY BETTER?

_____

_____

_____

NOTES:

_____

_____

_____

_____

_____

_____

_____

Daily Wellness Journal

DATE: _____

WAKE UP	BED TIME	SLEEP (HRS)
_____	_____	_____

WHAT I ATE TODAY   EXERCISE LOG   PERSONAL ACTIVITIES

B _____   _____   _____

L _____   _____   _____

D _____   _____   _____

S _____   _____   _____

MOOD TRACKER   WATER INTAKE   FAMILY ACTIVITIES

◯ MORNING

◯ AFTERNOON

◯ NIGHT

_____

_____

_____

WHAT ARE YOU GRATEFUL FOR TODAY?   NOTES:

_____   _____

_____   _____

_____   _____

_____   _____

WHAT WOULD'VE MADE TODAY BETTER?   _____

_____   _____

_____   _____

_____   _____

Daily Wellness Journal

DATE: _____

WAKE UP	BED TIME	SLEEP (HRS)
_____	_____	_____

WHAT I ATE TODAY	EXERCISE LOG	PERSONAL ACTIVITIES
B _____	_____	_____
L _____	_____	_____
D _____	_____	_____
S _____	_____	_____

MOOD TRACKER

◯ MORNING

◯ AFTERNOON

◯ NIGHT

WATER INTAKE

FAMILY ACTIVITIES

_____

_____

_____

WHAT ARE YOU GRATEFUL FOR TODAY?

_____

_____

_____

WHAT WOULD'VE MADE TODAY BETTER?

_____

_____

_____

NOTES:

_____

_____

_____

_____

_____

_____

Daily Wellness Journal

DATE: _____

WAKE UP	BED TIME	SLEEP (HRS)
_____	_____	_____

WHAT I ATE TODAY

B _____

L _____

D _____

S _____

EXERCISE LOG

_____

_____

_____

_____

PERSONAL ACTIVITIES

_____

_____

_____

_____

MOOD TRACKER

◯ MORNING

◯ AFTERNOON

◯ NIGHT

WATER INTAKE

FAMILY ACTIVITIES

_____

_____

_____

WHAT ARE YOU GRATEFUL FOR TODAY?

_____

_____

_____

_____

WHAT WOULD'VE MADE TODAY BETTER?

_____

_____

_____

NOTES:

_____

_____

_____

_____

_____

_____

Daily Wellness Journal

DATE: _____

WAKE UP	BED TIME	SLEEP (HRS)
_____	_____	_____

WHAT I ATE TODAY / EXERCISE LOG / PERSONAL ACTIVITIES

WHAT I ATE TODAY	EXERCISE LOG	PERSONAL ACTIVITIES
B _____	_____	_____
L _____	_____	_____
D _____	_____	_____
S _____	_____	_____

MOOD TRACKER / WATER INTAKE / FAMILY ACTIVITIES

MOOD TRACKER

◯ MORNING

◯ AFTERNOON

◯ NIGHT

WATER INTAKE

FAMILY ACTIVITIES
_____
_____
_____

WHAT ARE YOU GRATEFUL FOR TODAY?
_____
_____
_____
_____

NOTES:
_____
_____
_____
_____
_____
_____

WHAT WOULD'VE MADE TODAY BETTER?
_____
_____
_____
_____

Daily Wellness Journal

DATE: _____

WAKE UP	BED TIME	SLEEP (HRS)
_____	_____	_____

WHAT I ATE TODAY	EXERCISE LOG	PERSONAL ACTIVITIES
B _____	_____	_____
L _____	_____	_____
D _____	_____	_____
S _____	_____	_____

MOOD TRACKER

◯ MORNING
◯ AFTERNOON
◯ NIGHT

WATER INTAKE

FAMILY ACTIVITIES

_____
_____
_____

WHAT ARE YOU GRATEFUL FOR TODAY?

_____
_____
_____

WHAT WOULD'VE MADE TODAY BETTER?

_____
_____
_____

NOTES:

_____
_____
_____
_____
_____
_____
_____
_____

Daily Wellness Journal

DATE: _____

WAKE UP	BED TIME	SLEEP (HRS)
_____	_____	_____

WHAT I ATE TODAY

B _____
L _____
D _____
S _____

EXERCISE LOG

_____
_____
_____
_____

PERSONAL ACTIVITIES

_____
_____
_____
_____

MOOD TRACKER

◯ MORNING
◯ AFTERNOON
◯ NIGHT

WATER INTAKE

FAMILY ACTIVITIES

_____
_____
_____

WHAT ARE YOU GRATEFUL FOR TODAY?

_____
_____
_____
_____

NOTES:

_____
_____
_____
_____
_____

WHAT WOULD'VE MADE TODAY BETTER?

_____
_____
_____

Daily Wellness Journal

DATE: _____

WAKE UP	BED TIME	SLEEP (HRS)
_____	_____	_____

WHAT I ATE TODAY   EXERCISE LOG   PERSONAL ACTIVITIES

B _____   _____   _____

L _____   _____   _____

D _____   _____   _____

S _____   _____   _____

MOOD TRACKER   WATER INTAKE   FAMILY ACTIVITIES

◯ MORNING

◯ AFTERNOON

◯ NIGHT

_____

_____

_____

WHAT ARE YOU GRATEFUL FOR TODAY?   NOTES:

_____   _____

_____   _____

_____   _____

_____   _____

WHAT WOULD'VE MADE TODAY BETTER?   _____

_____   _____

_____   _____

_____   _____

Daily Wellness Journal

DATE: _____

WAKE UP	BED TIME	SLEEP (HRS)
_____	_____	_____

WHAT I ATE TODAY

B _____

L _____

D _____

S _____

EXERCISE LOG

_____

_____

_____

_____

PERSONAL ACTIVITIES

_____

_____

_____

_____

MOOD TRACKER

◯ MORNING

◯ AFTERNOON

◯ NIGHT

WATER INTAKE

FAMILY ACTIVITIES

_____

_____

_____

WHAT ARE YOU GRATEFUL FOR TODAY?

_____

_____

_____

_____

WHAT WOULD'VE MADE TODAY BETTER?

_____

_____

_____

NOTES:

_____

_____

_____

_____

_____

_____

_____

_____

Daily Wellness Journal

DATE: _____

WAKE UP	BED TIME	SLEEP (HRS)
_____	_____	_____

WHAT I ATE TODAY

B _____
L _____
D _____
S _____

EXERCISE LOG

_____
_____
_____
_____

PERSONAL ACTIVITIES

_____
_____
_____
_____

MOOD TRACKER

◯ MORNING
◯ AFTERNOON
◯ NIGHT

WATER INTAKE

FAMILY ACTIVITIES

_____
_____
_____

WHAT ARE YOU GRATEFUL FOR TODAY?

_____
_____
_____
_____

WHAT WOULD'VE MADE TODAY BETTER?

_____
_____

NOTES:

_____
_____
_____
_____
_____
_____
_____
_____

Daily Wellness Journal

DATE: _____

WAKE UP	BED TIME	SLEEP (HRS)
_____	_____	_____

WHAT I ATE TODAY

B _____

L _____

D _____

S _____

EXERCISE LOG

_____

_____

_____

_____

PERSONAL ACTIVITIES

_____

_____

_____

_____

MOOD TRACKER

◯ MORNING

◯ AFTERNOON

◯ NIGHT

WATER INTAKE

FAMILY ACTIVITIES

_____

_____

_____

WHAT ARE YOU GRATEFUL FOR TODAY?

_____

_____

_____

_____

WHAT WOULD'VE MADE TODAY BETTER?

_____

_____

_____

NOTES:

_____

_____

_____

_____

_____

_____

_____

_____

_____

Daily Wellness Journal

DATE: _____

WAKE UP	BED TIME	SLEEP (HRS)
_____	_____	_____

WHAT I ATE TODAY

B _____

L _____

D _____

S _____

EXERCISE LOG

_____

_____

_____

_____

PERSONAL ACTIVITIES

_____

_____

_____

_____

MOOD TRACKER

◯ MORNING

◯ AFTERNOON

◯ NIGHT

WATER INTAKE

FAMILY ACTIVITIES

_____

_____

_____

WHAT ARE YOU GRATEFUL FOR TODAY?

_____

_____

_____

_____

WHAT WOULD'VE MADE TODAY BETTER?

_____

_____

_____

NOTES:

_____

_____

_____

_____

_____

_____

_____

_____

Daily Wellness Journal

DATE: _____

WAKE UP	BED TIME	SLEEP (HRS)
_____	_____	_____

WHAT I ATE TODAY

B _____

L _____

D _____

S _____

EXERCISE LOG

_____

_____

_____

_____

PERSONAL ACTIVITIES

_____

_____

_____

_____

MOOD TRACKER

◯ MORNING

◯ AFTERNOON

◯ NIGHT

WATER INTAKE

FAMILY ACTIVITIES

_____

_____

_____

WHAT ARE YOU GRATEFUL FOR TODAY?

_____

_____

_____

_____

WHAT WOULD'VE MADE TODAY BETTER?

_____

_____

_____

NOTES:

_____

_____

_____

_____

_____

_____

Daily Wellness Journal

DATE: _____

WAKE UP	BED TIME	SLEEP (HRS)
_____	_____	_____

WHAT I ATE TODAY	EXERCISE LOG	PERSONAL ACTIVITIES
B _____	_____	_____
L _____	_____	_____
D _____	_____	_____
S _____	_____	_____

MOOD TRACKER

- ◯ MORNING
- ◯ AFTERNOON
- ◯ NIGHT

WATER INTAKE

FAMILY ACTIVITIES

_____

_____

_____

_____

WHAT ARE YOU GRATEFUL FOR TODAY?

_____

_____

_____

_____

WHAT WOULD'VE MADE TODAY BETTER?

_____

_____

_____

_____

NOTES:

_____

_____

_____

_____

_____

_____

_____

_____

_____

Daily Wellness Journal

DATE: _____

WAKE UP	BED TIME	SLEEP (HRS)
_____	_____	_____

WHAT I ATE TODAY   EXERCISE LOG   PERSONAL ACTIVITIES

B _____   _____   _____

L _____   _____   _____

D _____   _____   _____

S _____   _____   _____

MOOD TRACKER   WATER INTAKE   FAMILY ACTIVITIES

◯ MORNING

◯ AFTERNOON

◯ NIGHT

WHAT ARE YOU GRATEFUL FOR TODAY?   NOTES:

_____

_____

_____

_____

WHAT WOULD'VE MADE TODAY BETTER?

_____

_____

_____

Daily Wellness Journal

DATE: _____

WAKE UP	BED TIME	SLEEP (HRS)
_____	_____	_____

WHAT I ATE TODAY	EXERCISE LOG	PERSONAL ACTIVITIES
B _____	_____	_____
L _____	_____	_____
D _____	_____	_____
S _____	_____	_____

MOOD TRACKER

◯ MORNING
◯ AFTERNOON
◯ NIGHT

WATER INTAKE

FAMILY ACTIVITIES
_____
_____
_____

WHAT ARE YOU GRATEFUL FOR TODAY?
_____
_____
_____
_____

WHAT WOULD'VE MADE TODAY BETTER?
_____
_____
_____

NOTES:
_____
_____
_____
_____
_____
_____
_____
_____

Daily Wellness Journal

DATE: _____

WAKE UP	BED TIME	SLEEP (HRS)
_____	_____	_____

WHAT I ATE TODAY

B _____

L _____

D _____

S _____

EXERCISE LOG

_____

_____

_____

_____

PERSONAL ACTIVITIES

_____

_____

_____

_____

MOOD TRACKER

◯ MORNING

◯ AFTERNOON

◯ NIGHT

WATER INTAKE

FAMILY ACTIVITIES

_____

_____

_____

WHAT ARE YOU GRATEFUL FOR TODAY?

_____

_____

_____

_____

WHAT WOULD'VE MADE TODAY BETTER?

_____

_____

_____

NOTES:

_____

_____

_____

_____

_____

_____

_____

_____

Daily Wellness Journal

DATE: _____

WAKE UP	BED TIME	SLEEP (HRS)
_____	_____	_____

WHAT I ATE TODAY   EXERCISE LOG   PERSONAL ACTIVITIES

B _____   _____   _____

L _____   _____   _____

D _____   _____   _____

S _____   _____   _____

MOOD TRACKER   WATER INTAKE   FAMILY ACTIVITIES

◯ MORNING

◯ AFTERNOON

◯ NIGHT

_____

_____

_____

WHAT ARE YOU GRATEFUL FOR TODAY?   NOTES:

_____   _____

_____   _____

_____   _____

_____   _____

WHAT WOULD'VE MADE TODAY BETTER?

_____   _____

_____   _____

_____   _____

Daily Wellness Journal

DATE: _____

WAKE UP	BED TIME	SLEEP (HRS)
_____	_____	_____

WHAT I ATE TODAY	EXERCISE LOG	PERSONAL ACTIVITIES
B _____	_____	_____
L _____	_____	_____
D _____	_____	_____
S _____	_____	_____

MOOD TRACKER	WATER INTAKE	FAMILY ACTIVITIES
◯ MORNING		_____
◯ AFTERNOON		_____
◯ NIGHT		_____

WHAT ARE YOU GRATEFUL FOR TODAY?

_____

_____

_____

_____

WHAT WOULD'VE MADE TODAY BETTER?

_____

_____

_____

NOTES:

_____

_____

_____

_____

_____

_____

Daily Wellness Journal

DATE: _____

WAKE UP	BED TIME	SLEEP (HRS)
_____	_____	_____

WHAT I ATE TODAY / EXERCISE LOG / PERSONAL ACTIVITIES

B _____ _____ _____

L _____ _____ _____

D _____ _____ _____

S _____ _____ _____

MOOD TRACKER

◯ MORNING

◯ AFTERNOON

◯ NIGHT

WATER INTAKE

FAMILY ACTIVITIES

_____

_____

_____

_____

WHAT ARE YOU GRATEFUL FOR TODAY?

_____

_____

_____

_____

WHAT WOULD'VE MADE TODAY BETTER?

_____

_____

_____

NOTES:

_____

_____

_____

_____

_____

_____

_____

Daily Wellness Journal

DATE: _____

WAKE UP	BED TIME	SLEEP (HRS)
_____	_____	_____

WHAT I ATE TODAY / EXERCISE LOG / PERSONAL ACTIVITIES

WHAT I ATE TODAY	EXERCISE LOG	PERSONAL ACTIVITIES
B _____	_____	_____
L _____	_____	_____
D _____	_____	_____
S _____	_____	_____

MOOD TRACKER / WATER INTAKE / FAMILY ACTIVITIES

MOOD TRACKER
- ◯ MORNING
- ◯ AFTERNOON
- ◯ NIGHT

WATER INTAKE

FAMILY ACTIVITIES
- _____
- _____
- _____

WHAT ARE YOU GRATEFUL FOR TODAY?

_____

_____

_____

_____

WHAT WOULD'VE MADE TODAY BETTER?

_____

_____

_____

NOTES:

_____

_____

_____

_____

_____

_____

_____

Daily Wellness Journal

DATE: _____

WAKE UP	BED TIME	SLEEP (HRS)
_____	_____	_____

WHAT I ATE TODAY

B _____

L _____

D _____

S _____

EXERCISE LOG

_____

_____

_____

_____

PERSONAL ACTIVITIES

_____

_____

_____

_____

MOOD TRACKER

◯ MORNING

◯ AFTERNOON

◯ NIGHT

WATER INTAKE

FAMILY ACTIVITIES

_____

_____

_____

_____

WHAT ARE YOU GRATEFUL FOR TODAY?

_____

_____

_____

_____

WHAT WOULD'VE MADE TODAY BETTER?

_____

_____

_____

NOTES:

_____

_____

_____

_____

_____

_____

_____

_____

_____

Daily Wellness Journal

DATE: _____

WAKE UP	BED TIME	SLEEP (HRS)
_____	_____	_____

WHAT I ATE TODAY   EXERCISE LOG   PERSONAL ACTIVITIES

B _____   _____   _____

L _____   _____   _____

D _____   _____   _____

S _____   _____   _____

MOOD TRACKER   WATER INTAKE   FAMILY ACTIVITIES

◯ MORNING

◯ AFTERNOON

◯ NIGHT

WHAT ARE YOU GRATEFUL FOR TODAY?   NOTES:

_____

_____

_____

_____

WHAT WOULD'VE MADE TODAY BETTER?

_____

_____

_____

Daily Wellness Journal

DATE: _____

WAKE UP	BED TIME	SLEEP (HRS)
_____	_____	_____

WHAT I ATE TODAY

B _____

L _____

D _____

S _____

EXERCISE LOG

_____

_____

_____

_____

PERSONAL ACTIVITIES

_____

_____

_____

_____

MOOD TRACKER

◯ MORNING

◯ AFTERNOON

◯ NIGHT

WATER INTAKE

FAMILY ACTIVITIES

_____

_____

_____

_____

WHAT ARE YOU GRATEFUL FOR TODAY?

_____

_____

_____

_____

NOTES:

_____

_____

_____

_____

_____

_____

WHAT WOULD'VE MADE TODAY BETTER?

_____

_____

_____

Daily Wellness Journal

DATE: _____

WAKE UP	BED TIME	SLEEP (HRS)
_____	_____	_____

WHAT I ATE TODAY

B _____

L _____

D _____

S _____

EXERCISE LOG

_____

_____

_____

_____

PERSONAL ACTIVITIES

_____

_____

_____

MOOD TRACKER

◯ MORNING

◯ AFTERNOON

◯ NIGHT

WATER INTAKE

FAMILY ACTIVITIES

_____

_____

_____

WHAT ARE YOU GRATEFUL FOR TODAY?

_____

_____

_____

_____

WHAT WOULD'VE MADE TODAY BETTER?

_____

_____

_____

NOTES:

_____

_____

_____

_____

_____

_____

_____

_____

Daily Wellness Journal

DATE: _____

WAKE UP	BED TIME	SLEEP (HRS)
_____	_____	_____

WHAT I ATE TODAY

B _____

L _____

D _____

S _____

EXERCISE LOG

_____

_____

_____

_____

PERSONAL ACTIVITIES

_____

_____

_____

_____

MOOD TRACKER

◯ MORNING

◯ AFTERNOON

◯ NIGHT

WATER INTAKE

FAMILY ACTIVITIES

_____

_____

_____

_____

WHAT ARE YOU GRATEFUL FOR TODAY?

_____

_____

_____

_____

WHAT WOULD'VE MADE TODAY BETTER?

_____

_____

_____

NOTES:

_____

_____

_____

_____

_____

_____

_____

_____

Daily Wellness Journal

DATE: _____

WAKE UP	BED TIME	SLEEP (HRS)
_____	_____	_____

WHAT I ATE TODAY   EXERCISE LOG   PERSONAL ACTIVITIES

B _____   _____   _____

L _____   _____   _____

D _____   _____   _____

S _____   _____   _____

MOOD TRACKER   WATER INTAKE   FAMILY ACTIVITIES

◯ MORNING

◯ AFTERNOON

◯ NIGHT

FAMILY ACTIVITIES
_____
_____
_____

WHAT ARE YOU GRATEFUL FOR TODAY?   NOTES:
_____   _____
_____   _____
_____   _____
_____   _____
                          _____

WHAT WOULD'VE MADE TODAY BETTER?
_____   _____
_____   _____
_____   _____

Daily Wellness Journal

DATE: _____

WAKE UP	BED TIME	SLEEP (HRS)
_____	_____	_____

WHAT I ATE TODAY

B _____

L _____

D _____

S _____

EXERCISE LOG

_____

_____

_____

_____

PERSONAL ACTIVITIES

_____

_____

_____

_____

MOOD TRACKER

◯ MORNING

◯ AFTERNOON

◯ NIGHT

WATER INTAKE

FAMILY ACTIVITIES

_____

_____

_____

WHAT ARE YOU GRATEFUL FOR TODAY?

_____

_____

_____

_____

WHAT WOULD'VE MADE TODAY BETTER?

_____

_____

_____

NOTES:

_____

_____

_____

_____

_____

_____

_____

_____

_____

Daily Wellness Journal

DATE: _____

WAKE UP	BED TIME	SLEEP (HRS)
_____	_____	_____

WHAT I ATE TODAY   EXERCISE LOG   PERSONAL ACTIVITIES

B _____   _____   _____

L _____   _____   _____

D _____   _____   _____

S _____   _____   _____

MOOD TRACKER   WATER INTAKE   FAMILY ACTIVITIES

◯ MORNING

◯ AFTERNOON

◯ NIGHT

_____

_____

_____

WHAT ARE YOU GRATEFUL FOR TODAY?

_____

_____

_____

_____

WHAT WOULD'VE MADE TODAY BETTER?

_____

_____

_____

NOTES:

_____

_____

_____

_____

_____

_____

_____

_____

Daily Wellness Journal

DATE: _____

WAKE UP	BED TIME	SLEEP (HRS)
_____	_____	_____

WHAT I ATE TODAY

B _____

L _____

D _____

S _____

EXERCISE LOG

_____

_____

_____

_____

PERSONAL ACTIVITIES

_____

_____

_____

_____

MOOD TRACKER

◯ MORNING

◯ AFTERNOON

◯ NIGHT

WATER INTAKE

FAMILY ACTIVITIES

_____

_____

_____

_____

WHAT ARE YOU GRATEFUL FOR TODAY?

_____

_____

_____

_____

WHAT WOULD'VE MADE TODAY BETTER?

_____

_____

_____

NOTES:

_____

_____

_____

_____

_____

_____

_____

_____

Daily Wellness Journal

DATE: _____

WAKE UP	BED TIME	SLEEP (HRS)
_____	_____	_____

WHAT I ATE TODAY

B _____

L _____

D _____

S _____

EXERCISE LOG

_____

_____

_____

_____

PERSONAL ACTIVITIES

_____

_____

_____

_____

MOOD TRACKER

◯ MORNING

◯ AFTERNOON

◯ NIGHT

WATER INTAKE

FAMILY ACTIVITIES

_____

_____

_____

WHAT ARE YOU GRATEFUL FOR TODAY?

_____

_____

_____

_____

NOTES:

_____

_____

_____

_____

_____

_____

WHAT WOULD'VE MADE TODAY BETTER?

_____

_____

_____

Daily Wellness Journal

DATE: _____

WAKE UP	BED TIME	SLEEP (HRS)
_____	_____	_____

WHAT I ATE TODAY

B _____
L _____
D _____
S _____

EXERCISE LOG

_____
_____
_____
_____

PERSONAL ACTIVITIES

_____
_____
_____
_____

MOOD TRACKER

◯ MORNING
◯ AFTERNOON
◯ NIGHT

WATER INTAKE

FAMILY ACTIVITIES

_____
_____
_____

WHAT ARE YOU GRATEFUL FOR TODAY?

_____
_____
_____
_____

WHAT WOULD'VE MADE TODAY BETTER?

_____
_____
_____

NOTES:

_____
_____
_____
_____
_____
_____
_____
_____
_____

Daily Wellness Journal

DATE: _____

WAKE UP	BED TIME	SLEEP (HRS)
_____	_____	_____

WHAT I ATE TODAY | EXERCISE LOG | PERSONAL ACTIVITIES

B _____ _____ _____

L _____ _____ _____

D _____ _____ _____

S _____ _____ _____

MOOD TRACKER

◯ MORNING

◯ AFTERNOON

◯ NIGHT

WATER INTAKE

FAMILY ACTIVITIES

_____

_____

_____

WHAT ARE YOU GRATEFUL FOR TODAY?

_____

_____

_____

_____

WHAT WOULD'VE MADE TODAY BETTER?

_____

_____

_____

NOTES:

_____

_____

_____

_____

_____

_____

_____

_____

Daily Wellness Journal

DATE: _____

WAKE UP	BED TIME	SLEEP (HRS)
_____	_____	_____

WHAT I ATE TODAY	EXERCISE LOG	PERSONAL ACTIVITIES

B _____

L _____

D _____

S _____

MOOD TRACKER

◯ MORNING

◯ AFTERNOON

◯ NIGHT

WATER INTAKE

FAMILY ACTIVITIES

WHAT ARE YOU GRATEFUL FOR TODAY?

_____

_____

_____

_____

WHAT WOULD'VE MADE TODAY BETTER?

_____

_____

_____

NOTES:

_____

_____

_____

_____

_____

_____

_____

_____

Daily Wellness Journal

DATE: _____

WAKE UP	BED TIME	SLEEP (HRS)
_____	_____	_____

WHAT I ATE TODAY   EXERCISE LOG   PERSONAL ACTIVITIES

B _____   _____   _____

L _____   _____   _____

D _____   _____   _____

S _____   _____   _____

MOOD TRACKER   WATER INTAKE   FAMILY ACTIVITIES

◯ MORNING

◯ AFTERNOON

◯ NIGHT

_____

_____

_____

WHAT ARE YOU GRATEFUL FOR TODAY?   NOTES:

_____   _____

_____   _____

_____   _____

_____   _____

_____   _____

WHAT WOULD'VE MADE TODAY BETTER?   _____

_____   _____

_____   _____

_____   _____

_____   _____

Daily Wellness Journal

DATE: _____

WAKE UP	BED TIME	SLEEP (HRS)
_____	_____	_____

WHAT I ATE TODAY   EXERCISE LOG   PERSONAL ACTIVITIES

B _____   _____   _____

L _____   _____   _____

D _____   _____   _____

S _____   _____   _____

MOOD TRACKER   WATER INTAKE   FAMILY ACTIVITIES

◯ MORNING

◯ AFTERNOON

◯ NIGHT

WHAT ARE YOU GRATEFUL FOR TODAY?

_____

_____

_____

_____

WHAT WOULD'VE MADE TODAY BETTER?

_____

_____

_____

NOTES:

_____

_____

_____

_____

_____

_____

_____

_____

_____

Daily Wellness Journal

DATE: _____

WAKE UP	BED TIME	SLEEP (HRS)
_____	_____	_____

WHAT I ATE TODAY	EXERCISE LOG	PERSONAL ACTIVITIES
B _____	_____	_____
L _____	_____	_____
D _____	_____	_____
S _____	_____	_____

MOOD TRACKER	WATER INTAKE	FAMILY ACTIVITIES
◯ MORNING		_____
◯ AFTERNOON		_____
◯ NIGHT		_____

WHAT ARE YOU GRATEFUL FOR TODAY?

_____

_____

_____

_____

WHAT WOULD'VE MADE TODAY BETTER?

_____

_____

_____

NOTES:

_____

_____

_____

_____

_____

_____

Daily Wellness Journal

DATE: _____

WAKE UP	BED TIME	SLEEP (HRS)
_____	_____	_____

WHAT I ATE TODAY

B _____

L _____

D _____

S _____

EXERCISE LOG

_____

_____

_____

_____

PERSONAL ACTIVITIES

_____

_____

_____

_____

MOOD TRACKER

◯ MORNING

◯ AFTERNOON

◯ NIGHT

WATER INTAKE

FAMILY ACTIVITIES

_____

_____

_____

_____

WHAT ARE YOU GRATEFUL FOR TODAY?

_____

_____

_____

_____

WHAT WOULD'VE MADE TODAY BETTER?

_____

_____

_____

NOTES:

_____

_____

_____

_____

_____

_____

_____

_____

_____

Daily Wellness Journal

DATE: _____

WAKE UP	BED TIME	SLEEP (HRS)
_____	_____	_____

WHAT I ATE TODAY   EXERCISE LOG   PERSONAL ACTIVITIES

B _____ _____ _____

L _____ _____ _____

D _____ _____ _____

S _____ _____ _____

MOOD TRACKER   WATER INTAKE   FAMILY ACTIVITIES

◯ MORNING

◯ AFTERNOON

◯ NIGHT

WHAT ARE YOU GRATEFUL FOR TODAY?

_____

_____

_____

_____

WHAT WOULD'VE MADE TODAY BETTER?

_____

_____

_____

NOTES:

_____

_____

_____

_____

_____

_____

_____

Daily Wellness Journal

DATE: _____

WAKE UP	BED TIME	SLEEP (HRS)
_____	_____	_____

WHAT I ATE TODAY

B _____

L _____

D _____

S _____

EXERCISE LOG

_____

_____

_____

_____

PERSONAL ACTIVITIES

_____

_____

_____

_____

MOOD TRACKER

◯ MORNING

◯ AFTERNOON

◯ NIGHT

WATER INTAKE

FAMILY ACTIVITIES

_____

_____

_____

WHAT ARE YOU GRATEFUL FOR TODAY?

_____

_____

_____

_____

WHAT WOULD'VE MADE TODAY BETTER?

_____

_____

_____

NOTES:

_____

_____

_____

_____

_____

_____

_____

_____

Daily Wellness Journal

DATE: _____

WAKE UP	BED TIME	SLEEP (HRS)
_____	_____	_____

WHAT I ATE TODAY	EXERCISE LOG	PERSONAL ACTIVITIES
B _____	_____	_____
L _____	_____	_____
D _____	_____	_____
S _____	_____	_____

MOOD TRACKER

◯ MORNING

◯ AFTERNOON

◯ NIGHT

WATER INTAKE

FAMILY ACTIVITIES

_____

_____

_____

WHAT ARE YOU GRATEFUL FOR TODAY?

_____

_____

_____

_____

WHAT WOULD'VE MADE TODAY BETTER?

_____

_____

_____

NOTES:

_____

_____

_____

_____

_____

_____

_____

Daily Wellness Journal

DATE: _____

WAKE UP	BED TIME	SLEEP (HRS)
_____	_____	_____

WHAT I ATE TODAY

B _____

L _____

D _____

S _____

EXERCISE LOG

_____

_____

_____

_____

PERSONAL ACTIVITIES

_____

_____

_____

_____

MOOD TRACKER

◯ MORNING

◯ AFTERNOON

◯ NIGHT

WATER INTAKE

FAMILY ACTIVITIES

_____

_____

_____

WHAT ARE YOU GRATEFUL FOR TODAY?

_____

_____

_____

_____

WHAT WOULD'VE MADE TODAY BETTER?

_____

_____

_____

NOTES:

_____

_____

_____

_____

_____

_____

_____

Daily Wellness Journal

DATE: _____

WAKE UP	BED TIME	SLEEP (HRS)
_____	_____	_____

WHAT I ATE TODAY	EXERCISE LOG	PERSONAL ACTIVITIES
B _____	_____	_____
L _____	_____	_____
D _____	_____	_____
S _____	_____	_____

MOOD TRACKER

◯ MORNING
◯ AFTERNOON
◯ NIGHT

WATER INTAKE

FAMILY ACTIVITIES

_____

_____

_____

WHAT ARE YOU GRATEFUL FOR TODAY?

_____

_____

_____

_____

WHAT WOULD'VE MADE TODAY BETTER?

_____

_____

_____

NOTES:

_____

_____

_____

_____

_____

_____

_____

_____

Daily Wellness Journal

DATE: _____

WAKE UP	BED TIME	SLEEP (HRS)
_____	_____	_____

WHAT I ATE TODAY

B _____

L _____

D _____

S _____

EXERCISE LOG

_____

_____

_____

_____

PERSONAL ACTIVITIES

_____

_____

_____

_____

MOOD TRACKER

◯ MORNING

◯ AFTERNOON

◯ NIGHT

WATER INTAKE

FAMILY ACTIVITIES

_____

_____

_____

WHAT ARE YOU GRATEFUL FOR TODAY?

_____

_____

_____

_____

WHAT WOULD'VE MADE TODAY BETTER?

_____

_____

_____

NOTES:

_____

_____

_____

_____

_____

_____

_____

_____

Daily Wellness Journal

DATE: _____

WAKE UP	BED TIME	SLEEP (HRS)
_____	_____	_____

WHAT I ATE TODAY	EXERCISE LOG	PERSONAL ACTIVITIES
B _____	_____	_____
L _____	_____	_____
D _____	_____	_____
S _____	_____	_____

MOOD TRACKER

◯ MORNING

◯ AFTERNOON

◯ NIGHT

WATER INTAKE

FAMILY ACTIVITIES

_____

_____

WHAT ARE YOU GRATEFUL FOR TODAY?

_____

_____

_____

_____

WHAT WOULD'VE MADE TODAY BETTER?

_____

_____

_____

NOTES:

_____

_____

_____

_____

_____

_____

_____

_____

Daily Wellness Journal

DATE: _____

WAKE UP	BED TIME	SLEEP (HRS)
_____	_____	_____

WHAT I ATE TODAY

B _____

L _____

D _____

S _____

EXERCISE LOG

_____

_____

_____

_____

PERSONAL ACTIVITIES

_____

_____

_____

_____

MOOD TRACKER

◯ MORNING

◯ AFTERNOON

◯ NIGHT

WATER INTAKE

FAMILY ACTIVITIES

_____

_____

_____

_____

WHAT ARE YOU GRATEFUL FOR TODAY?

_____

_____

_____

_____

WHAT WOULD'VE MADE TODAY BETTER?

_____

_____

_____

NOTES:

_____

_____

_____

_____

_____

_____

_____

_____

Daily Wellness Journal

DATE: _____

WAKE UP	BED TIME	SLEEP (HRS)
_____	_____	_____

WHAT I ATE TODAY

B _____

L _____

D _____

S _____

EXERCISE LOG

_____

_____

_____

_____

PERSONAL ACTIVITIES

_____

_____

_____

_____

MOOD TRACKER

◯ MORNING

◯ AFTERNOON

◯ NIGHT

WATER INTAKE

FAMILY ACTIVITIES

_____

_____

_____

WHAT ARE YOU GRATEFUL FOR TODAY?

_____

_____

_____

_____

WHAT WOULD'VE MADE TODAY BETTER?

_____

_____

_____

NOTES:

_____

_____

_____

_____

_____

_____

_____

_____

Daily Wellness Journal

DATE: _____

WAKE UP	BED TIME	SLEEP (HRS)
_____	_____	_____

WHAT I ATE TODAY   EXERCISE LOG   PERSONAL ACTIVITIES

B _____   _____   _____

L _____   _____   _____

D _____   _____   _____

S _____   _____   _____

MOOD TRACKER   WATER INTAKE   FAMILY ACTIVITIES

◯ MORNING

◯ AFTERNOON

◯ NIGHT

WHAT ARE YOU GRATEFUL FOR TODAY?

_____

_____

_____

WHAT WOULD'VE MADE TODAY BETTER?

_____

_____

_____

NOTES:

_____

_____

_____

_____

_____

Daily Wellness Journal

DATE: _____

WAKE UP	BED TIME	SLEEP (HRS)
_____	_____	_____

WHAT I ATE TODAY

B _____

L _____

D _____

S _____

EXERCISE LOG

_____

_____

_____

_____

PERSONAL ACTIVITIES

_____

_____

_____

_____

MOOD TRACKER

◯ MORNING

◯ AFTERNOON

◯ NIGHT

WATER INTAKE

FAMILY ACTIVITIES

_____

_____

_____

WHAT ARE YOU GRATEFUL FOR TODAY?

_____

_____

_____

_____

NOTES:

_____

_____

_____

_____

_____

_____

WHAT WOULD'VE MADE TODAY BETTER?

_____

_____

_____

_____

Daily Wellness Journal

DATE: _____

WAKE UP	BED TIME	SLEEP (HRS)
_____	_____	_____

WHAT I ATE TODAY   EXERCISE LOG   PERSONAL ACTIVITIES

B _____ _____ _____

L _____ _____ _____

D _____ _____ _____

S _____ _____ _____

MOOD TRACKER   WATER INTAKE   FAMILY ACTIVITIES

◯ MORNING

◯ AFTERNOON

◯ NIGHT

_____

_____

_____

WHAT ARE YOU GRATEFUL FOR TODAY?

_____

_____

_____

_____

WHAT WOULD'VE MADE TODAY BETTER?

_____

_____

_____

NOTES:

_____

_____

_____

_____

_____

_____

_____

Geico. Com
 ↳ Menu
  ↳ insurance
   ↳ vehicle insurance
    ↳ "Mexico Auto"

286. — oa Price 2 Kits
+ 13.54   tax
+ 14.95   S + H
_____   Total
314.49
- 88.00   ←Refund
-   3.79   Auto tax Refund
_____
  222.70 (This is - tax)

Per Admin, it's $226.49 in the
balance which is w/out the tax deduction of 3.79

tax rate 4.50%

286 - 88 = New price = $198 } $8.91
    just kits